Module 2: Group Work & Projects

Introduction

In higher education, it is necessary to participate in collaborative projects, and group work is an integral part of many courses. The skills you need to develop in order to work effectively in group projects and participate in group discussions are vital for success at university. They are equally important in many professions. This module focuses on what is involved in effective group work and how you can engage successfully in these situations. The tasks practise working in groups to complete a group project. You will understand the key stages involved, from planning to implementation to evaluation of group performance. At the end of this module, you will understand what is expected of you in assessed group work and you will also be able to participate more confidently in group discussions, using appropriate language.

Contents

1 What is *group work* and why is it important?

At the end of this unit, you will be able to:

- identify the key features of group work
- recognise the benefits and challenges of group work
- identify the skills required for effective group work and how it is assessed
- analyse the requirements of a set group project task

Task 1 What is *group work*?

Group work involves working with other students to complete one or more tasks in order to develop a final project outcome. For example, your group may be required to deliver a presentation, design a prototype or produce a video.

A group project usually involves a series of tasks to be completed over several weeks by a set deadline. You could, for example, be required to conduct a survey, analyse the data collected, report your findings in an oral presentation and, finally, write a report.

Your lecturer may allocate you to a specific group, in which case, it is likely you will be working on the project with people you do not know well, or you may be allowed to choose your own group members. Group size depends on the project itself, but can range from as few as three group members to ten or more.

In order to effectively complete the group project in this module, each group will need to meet regularly away from the classroom to plan, organise and review the project. All members of the group will need to contribute to the planning, research and presentation of findings. You will also need to work informally in groups in order to have discussions and complete practical work.

Almost all undergraduate courses will have at least one assessed group project, which means you will be allocated a mark or grade for your contribution to the project. You may be assessed on the process or on the final assignment, or both.

In this module, you will work in groups to:

- produce a poster
- prepare for and participate in a debate

and individually to:

- write a reflective report on the process

1.1 **Are the statements true (T) or false (F)? Compare your answers with a partner's.**

a. Lecturers in UK universities often ask students to work together in groups. ☐
b. Group projects can include several stages. ☐
c. Groups self-select their members. ☐
d. All elements of group projects are marked. ☐
e. Groups are expected to meet in their own time. ☐
f. The maximum group size is ten students. ☐

1.2 **What has been your experience of group-work assignments or group projects? Discuss the questions with a partner. Make a note of your answers and be prepared to present them to the class.**

a. What did you have to do?

b. How were the group members selected?

c. How was the assignment or project marked?

d. What guidance were you given on how to work in groups?

e. How did you manage any conflicts between the members?

1

Task 2 Why group work?

Universities are including more group work in their courses for two main reasons:

1. Working in groups can lead to rich learning experiences; working together effectively means gaining from the group – learning with and from your peers.
2. Learning to work effectively with others is an important skill that is highly prized in the workplace.

Working in a group can present challenges to all its members, especially if you have had no experience of it before. You may not know what is expected of you or how to contribute as much as you should.

2.1 Work in groups. You are going to take part in and evaluate a short group activity. Your tutor will provide each group with an object.

In your group, think of an alternative use for the object and complete the table.

name of object	
use	
marketability	
price/value	
durability	

2.2 Give a short group presentation in which you introduce your object and promote it. The other groups will vote on the most creative idea.

2.3 Discuss the questions with your group.

a. What role did you have in the discussion and presentation?
b. Did all the members of the group contribute or did some members dominate?
c. Who came up with the various ideas?
d. Did you agree with the final outcome, or would you have preferred a different result?
e. How effectively did your group work as a team?
f. How effective was the final presentation?

2.4 **Working in groups presents both challenges and valuable learning opportunities. Work with a partner to rank the benefits of group work in order of importance to you.**

Use a scale of 1 to 9 (1 = most important, 9 = least important).

Working in groups on a project allows me to:

a. work with students from different cultural backgrounds ___

b. learn from other students in the group ___

c. develop important communication skills ___

d. share the workload ___

e. get to know a small group of students socially ___

f. gain new perspectives on study topics ___

g. develop my time management skills ___

h. discover my specific strengths as a team player ___

i. learn how to deal with challenge and conflict ___

2.5 **Complete a skills audit. In order to work effectively in a group project, you will need to develop certain skills. Which of the skills below do you need to develop? Put a mark on the line to show your answer.**

a. contributing to discussions

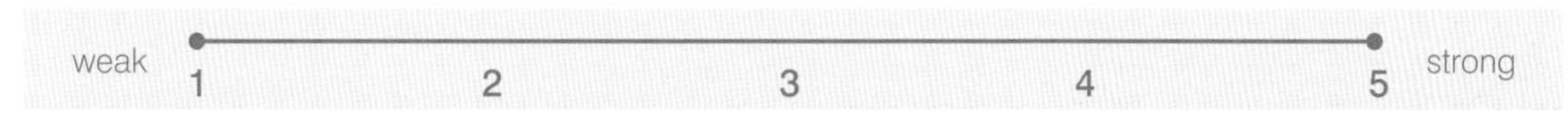

b. planning and organising group meetings

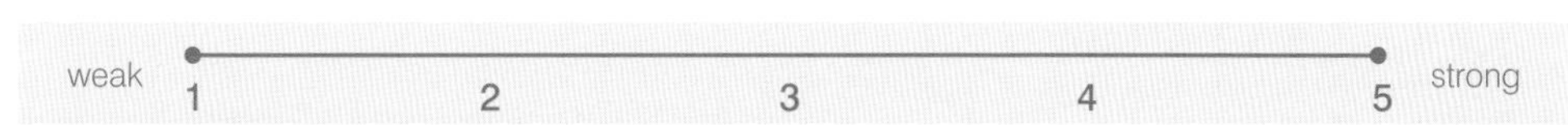

c. listening actively

d. getting your point across clearly to your audience

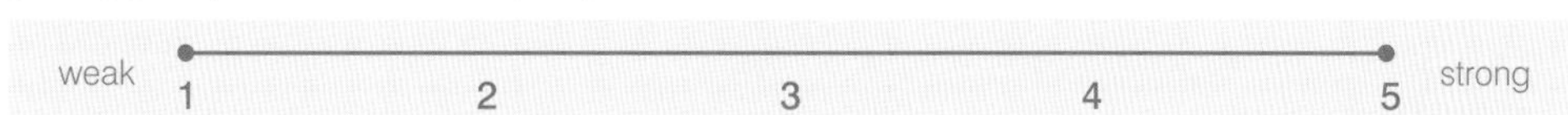

e. understanding body language (non-verbal communication)

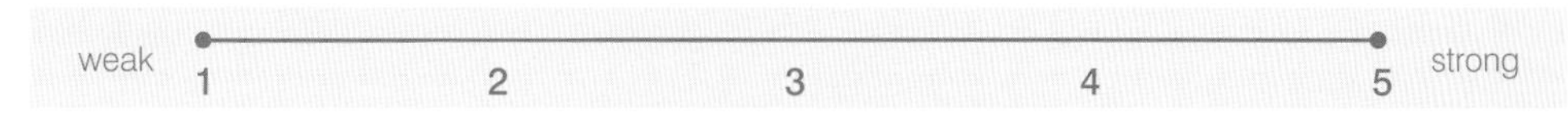

f. giving and receiving helpful criticism or constructive feedback

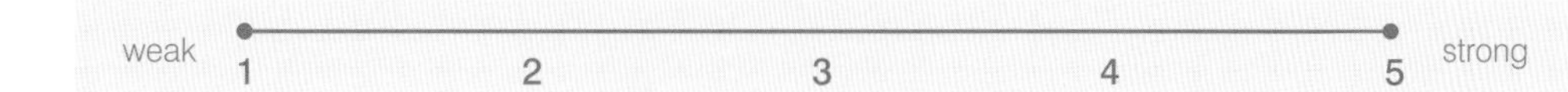

You will evaluate your skills again at the end of the module to assess the extent to which you have developed each skill.

Task 3 Assessment of group work

You will develop skills *and* acquire subject knowledge by engaging in group projects. Group work is, therefore, often assessed on more than one level. Your tutors are interested in the stages you go through as a group from the start of the project to the finished product (the final assignment). Of course, you will need to produce a good assignment, on time, but tutors will also assess you on the process.

3.1 Match the assessment types (a–e) with the correct assessment brief (1–5).

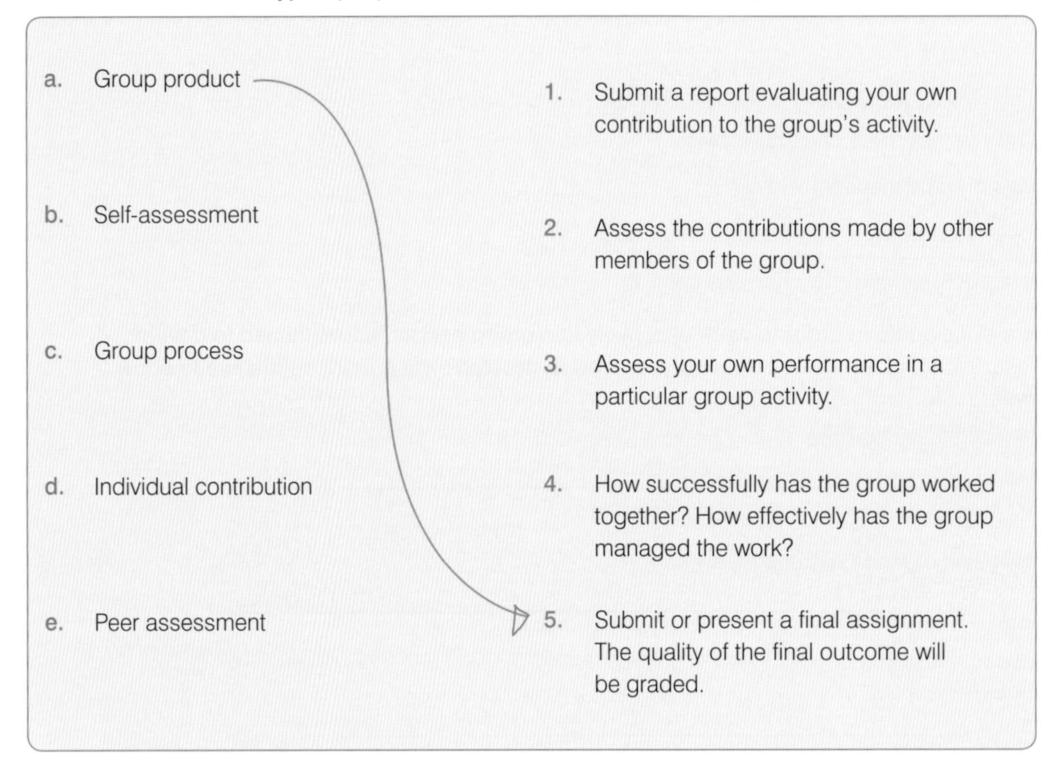

a. Group product

b. Self-assessment

c. Group process

d. Individual contribution

e. Peer assessment

1. Submit a report evaluating your own contribution to the group's activity.
2. Assess the contributions made by other members of the group.
3. Assess your own performance in a particular group activity.
4. How successfully has the group worked together? How effectively has the group managed the work?
5. Submit or present a final assignment. The quality of the final outcome will be graded.

Task 4 Project brief

4.1 Read the project brief carefully.

Project Brief: Endangered Species

In this project, you are required to:
- produce a poster
- prepare for and participate in a debate
- write a reflective report on the process

You will be divided into groups of four or five to produce the poster and prepare for the debate. You will then be required to work independently to write a report on the process. You are encouraged to work together and support each other through the process of the project. You will need to be self-motivated as well as share in joint decisions of your group. Your tutor will provide deadlines for each element of the project.

Assessment

You will be assessed on:
- the effectiveness of your contribution to the group project, when working on the poster and the debate
- your ability to evaluate the collaborative process, when writing the reflective report

Learning outcomes

The project aims to develop the following skills:
- teamwork
- guided independent study
- research skills
- report writing
- presentation skills
- decision making

Project stages

1. Poster

Work with your group to produce a poster on an endangered species. Each group will present a different animal. You will respond to questions on the subject of your poster and on the process of collaboration.

Access the World Wildlife Fund (WWF) website (http://www.wwf.org.uk/wildlife/) for a list of animals that are endangered, and choose an animal to research.

Include some of the following information on the endangered species in your poster presentation:

Description	• What do they look like? • What size are they? • How much do they weigh? • Do they have any distinguishing features?
Habitat	• Which part of the world do they live in? • Do they live in the jungle, desert, mountains, sea, etc.?
Food	• What do they eat?
Breeding	• Do they go anywhere specific to breed or lay eggs? • Do they have many young or a small number?
Threats	• Why are they endangered? • Is there just one major threat or are there several?
Conservation	• What can we do to protect these animals?

2. Debate

Debate topic: *Endangered species should be protected*. You are going to work in your groups to:
- research the topic
- come to a consensus on your position – for or against
- prepare for and carry out a debate

3. Report

Write a report of up to 500 words reflecting on the processes and outcomes of the project. Your report should address the question: *To what extent was your experience of working in a group successful?*

Source: Adapted from a project task authored by Jonathan Smith, ISLI, University of Reading.

The tasks in Units 2–6 will guide you through the process required to complete this group project successfully.

Reflect

What are your individual strengths? Think about how you can work effectively in your group and what you can contribute to this project.

2 Project planning

At the end of this unit, you will be able to:

- set goals and objectives
- plan and organise a group project
- collaborate to produce a poster

Task 1 Setting goals and objectives

Your group needs to have a clear idea of what you are expected to do to complete your project successfully. If you clarify your goals at the start of your project, you are more likely to be able to work together effectively.

1.1 **Reread the project brief on page 7 of Unit 1 again. Answer the questions and then discuss them with your group.**

a. What do you have to do?

b. How will the group members be selected?

c. How will the assignment be assessed?

d. What guidance will you receive?

Good project planning involves setting SMART goals. SMART is an acronym which stands for:
S – specific
M – measurable
A – achievable
R – relevant
T – timely

SMART goal criteria

specific	What specific information must be included to meet the requirements of the brief?
measurable	How will you know if your goal is successful? How will it be assessed?
achievable	Can you achieve your goal with the resources you have available?
relevant	Is the goal relevant to the final project outcome?
timely	When is the project goal due to be completed?

1.2 **Identify the three main goals of the group project and note these down.**

- *To produce a poster.*
- ______
- ______

1.3 **Are your main group project goals SMART goals? Apply the SMART goal criteria to each goal. Rewrite your group project goals as SMART goals, if necessary.**

Example

- *Our first goal is to design and produce a poster by [date] that features one endangered species.*

It is important to break down your goals into a list of objectives; these are the tasks that need to be completed in order to achieve each goal.

1.4 **Work with a partner to brainstorm a list of objectives your group will need to complete in order to produce a poster.**

1.5 **Compare your list with the Project Planning checklist below. Add additional tasks to the list if necessary, then number the steps in the order you will conduct them.**

Project Planning checklist

- Design the poster layout – what will the finished poster look like? ___
- Type up text for each section: description, habitat, etc. ___
- Gather information for the poster presentation. ___
- Find suitable graphics/images. ___
- Choose your topic. Which endangered species will you present on your poster? 1
- Proofread and edit text and graphics. ___
- Prepare a mock-up (first draft) of your poster. ___
- Check you understand the assessment criteria. ___
- ______________________ ___
- ______________________ ___
- ______________________ ___
- ______________________ ___
- ______________________ ___

2

Task 2 Organising your group project

Now that you know what you have to do, you need to allocate tasks and share responsibilities across all members of the group. It is worthwhile taking the time to get to know the other members of your group before allocating roles.

It is important that every member of your group takes responsibility for the project as a whole, but different elements of the project can be assigned to individuals. How can the work be divided between the members of the group? You need to work together and agree to take responsibility for different aspects of the project, making sure that each member contributes.

2.1 Introduce yourself to your group and answer the questions.

a. Have you worked in a group before?

____

b. If so, what worked well and what was not effective?

____

c. What makes you a good team member?

____

d. What skills can you contribute?

____

2.2 Based on individual strengths, decide who should take on the role of group coordinator and the role of group secretary.

Group Coordinator: To review the overall progress on the poster preparation, to lead meetings, to chair discussion prior to a seminar.

Group Secretary: To prepare an agenda for each meeting, to take notes in meetings, to circulate action items to the group.

2.3 How will your group communicate throughout the project? Make a list of names and contact details. Exchange these contact details with all members of the group.

name	email	phone number

Arrange to meet the other members of your group regularly. Plan in advance when and where you will meet and note these appointments in your calendar.

It is not always possible to meet face-to-face with other people in your group, because you have other commitments. In this case, consider using online tools, such as those listed in Task 2.4, which enable you to communicate and collaborate with others over the internet. At the very least, you will need to create a shared digital platform where files and documents can be stored and shared.

2.4 **Work in groups. Assign each member one of the online collaborative tools in the table below. Access and review your tool. Complete the table and present the information to your group at your first meeting.**

online collaborative tool	main features	advantages	disadvantages
Google Docs This is a free web-based service that you can use to collaborate on presentations and documents.			
Skype You can use this together with Google Docs to hold group chats as you can all see each other and talk together while you work on a task from different computers.			
join.me This tool lets you share your computer screen so that others can see it on a web browser or smartphone.			
meetings.io If you want to meet online with your team members without using a social network, you can use meetings.io.			

2

Task 3 Setting deadlines and allocating tasks

3.1 **Use the list of objectives you compiled in Task 1.5 to complete the table to create an implementation schedule.**

What needs to be done in order to prepare for the poster presentation?	When should it be done by?	Who is going to do it?

Another method of setting deadlines and allocating tasks is by creating a *Gantt chart*. This is a chart which displays this information in graphic form. This is useful to ensure your group is on track and able to meet the deadlines set.

Produce a poster

Current period 7

Plan | Actual | % Complete | % Complete (beyond plan)

Tasks (to complete)	Plan start	Plan duration	Actual start	Actual duration	Per cent complete	Periods (week)											
						1	2	3	4	5	6	7	8	9	10	11	12
Select topic/species	1	1	1	1	100%												
Research																	
Description	2	4	2	3	100%												
Habitat	2	4	2	4	100%												
Food & Breeding	2	4	2	5	100%												
Threats & Conservation	2	4	2	3	100%												
Group meeting	3	1	3	1	100%												
Design poster layout	2	6	2	5	75%												
Type up the text	6	3	6	1	50%												
Find images/graphics	6	3	6	2	50%												
1st draft mock-up	9	1	9	1	0%												
Proofread & edit 1st draft	10	2	10	1	0%												

Task 4 Producing a poster

4.1 **Work in groups. Follow the guidance in this unit to plan and organise the design and delivery of the poster on an endangered species.**

- How will you shape the end product?
- Will different individual strengths suit different tasks to complete the project?
- What elements of the work will you be assessed on?
- Is there sufficient evidence of group collaboration?

4.2 **Exhibit your completed poster on the deadline and be prepared to answer questions on the content from your tutor and your classmates.**

Reflect

Keep a record of what is discussed at all meetings; these records will help you write the reflective report.

3 Preparing and presenting ideas in group discussions

At the end of this unit, you will:

- understand expectations for participating in group discussions
- research a discussion topic
- establish your point of view

Task 1 Advice for group discussions

1.1 **Read the advice for new students.**

> **Advice for new students**
>
> To get the most from a seminar or debate, you must prepare well. Make sure that you analyse the topic and think about it so you know what the main issues are, making notes as you go. Although seminars can take many different forms, everyone is expected to participate. You will need to find out in advance what the tutor requires for a seminar. For example, you could be expected to:
>
> - do some reading beforehand
> - give your opinions on the recommended reading
> - present a written paper
> - present a paper orally from notes
> - send a written version of your paper to everybody who will attend
> - lead a discussion
> - take part in a discussion with other students and the lecturer
> - summarise what has been said orally or in writing
> - hand in a written paper about a week after the seminar or tutorial
>
> Remember, seminars are for your benefit. You should prepare for seminars, making notes and summaries will help you to remember information and enable you to participate actively. The more actively you prepare and participate, the more you will learn.

1.2 **Are the statements true (T), false (F) or probably true (P), according to the text above? Where you are not sure, or if there is no information, put a question mark (?). Compare your answers with a partner's.**

a. Tutors organise seminars in advance and provide clear guidelines about what is expected of you. ☐
b. It is better to attend a seminar than miss it, even if you haven't prepared. ☐
c. You are all expected to contribute equally. ☐
d. Lack of preparation means that you probably won't learn anything in seminars. ☐
e. You should memorise what you are going to say before the seminar. ☐
f. You could prepare for a seminar with other students, sharing the work. ☐
g. At some point, you will need to do some writing. ☐
h. It is not necessary to do anything after a seminar. ☐

Task 2 Research the topic

2.1 **The topic for your debate is:** *Endangered species should be protected.* **Before you read the article in Task 2.3, in groups, spend a few minutes thinking about the topic.**

What are the positive and negative effects of animal conservation on endangered species, the environment and the local people?

Each person should think about a different aspect, for example, the positive impacts on the environment, or the negative impacts on the endangered species, and be prepared to share his/her ideas with the rest of the group.

2.2 **Work in groups to discuss your ideas and complete the table. Ideally, you should have short notes in each of the spaces in the table below at the end of this task.**

	positive impacts of animal conservation	negative impacts of animal conservation
an endangered species		
the environment		
the local people		

2.3 Read the article. It should give you some more ideas about the topic of animal conservation.

Wildlife conservation projects do more harm than good, says expert

New book claims Western-style schemes to protect animals damage the environment and criminalise local people

A new book claims that schemes to protect habitats of endangered animals, such as the Sumatran tiger, often end up criminalising local communities.

Ecotourism and Western-style conservation projects are harming wildlife, damaging the environment, and displacing and criminalising local people, according to a controversial new book.

The pristine beaches and wildlife tours demanded by overseas tourists has led to developments that do not benefit wildlife, such as beaches being built, mangroves stripped out, waterholes drilled and forests cleared, says Rosaleen Duffy, a world expert on the ethical dimensions of wildlife conservation and management.

These picture-perfect images all too often hide a 'darker history', she adds. Her new book, *Nature Crime: How We're Getting Conservation Wrong*, which draws on 15 years of research, 300 interviews with conservation professionals, local communities, tour operators and government officials, is published today.

When wildlife reserves are established, Duffy says, local communities can suddenly find that their everyday subsistence activities, such as hunting and collecting wood, have been outlawed.

At the same time, well-intentioned attempts to protect the habitats of animal species on the edge of extinction lead to the creation of wild, 'people-free' areas. This approach has led to the displacement of millions of people across the world.

'Conservation does not constitute neat win-win scenarios. Schemes come with rules and regulations that criminalise communities, dressed up in the language of partnership and participation, coupled with promises of new jobs in the tourism industry,' claims Duffy, professor of international politics at Manchester University.

A key failure of the Western-style conservation approach is the assumption that people are the enemies of wildlife conservation – that they are the illegal traders, the poachers, the hunters and the habitat destroyers. Equally flawed, she says, is the belief that those engaged in conservation are 'wildlife saviours'.

Such images, she argues, are oversimplifications. 'The inability to negotiate these conflicts and work with people on the ground is where conservation often sows the seeds of its own doom,' she adds.

'Why do some attempts to conserve wildlife end up pitting local communities against conservationists?' she asks. 'It is because they are regarded as unjust impositions, despite their good intentions. This is vital because failing to tackle such injustices damages wildlife conservation in the long run.'

Duffy stresses that her intention is not to persuade people to stop supporting conservation schemes. 'Wildlife is under threat and we need to act urgently,' she acknowledges. Instead, she says, she wants to encourage environmentalists to examine what the real costs and benefits of conservation are, so that better practices for people and for animals can be developed.

'The assumption that the ends justify the means results in a situation where the international conservation movement and their supporters around the world assume they are making ethical and environmentally sound decisions to save wildlife,' she says. 'In fact, they are supporting practices that have counterproductive, unethical and highly unjust outcomes.'

Duffy focuses on what she says is the fallacious belief that ecotourism is a solution to the problem of delivering economic development in an environmentally sustainable way.

This is, she says, a 'bewitchingly simple argument', but the assumption that such tourism necessarily translates into the kinds of development that benefits wildlife is far too simplistic.

'Holidaymakers are mostly unaware of how their tourist paradises have been produced,' she says. 'They assume that the picture-perfect landscape or the silver Caribbean beach is a natural feature. This is very far from the truth. Tourist playgrounds are manufactured environments, usually cleared of people. Similarly, hotel construction in tropical areas can result in clearing ecologically important mangroves or beach building which harms coral reefs.'

But the World Wildlife Fund for Nature, one of the four biggest environmental NGOs in the world, maintains that the loss of wildlife is one of the most important challenges facing our planet. As such, a powerful focus on conservation is necessary: 'Conservation is essential so let's not throw the baby out with the bathwater,' says a WWF-UK spokesman. 'There are examples out there where ecotourism is working and has thrown a lifeline to communities in terms of economics and social benefits, as well as added biodiversity benefits.

'Let's have more of those projects that are working for everybody and everything,' he adds. 'There is no one-size-fits-all when it comes to ecotourism and conservation.'

Source: http://www.theguardian.com/environment/2010/jul/29/wildlife-conservation-projects-more-harm

Task 3 Using thinking skills

3.1 **Did anything in the article in Task 2.3 surprise you? Why/Why not?**

3.2 **Use the ideas in the article in Task 2.3 to add more information to what you already know about issues related to animal conservation.**

Work in your groups. Arrange yourselves in pairs or groups of three. One person should refer to the text and suggest what the other(s) should note in the table below. All notes should be agreed.

Some points have been highlighted in the article and added to the table as examples.

P ➡ plus points (arguments and ideas for)	M ➡ minus points (arguments and ideas against)	I ➡ interesting points (arguments and ideas that don't easily fit into the other two columns)
• numbers of animals are in decline, e.g., the Sumatran tiger	• may criminalise local communities who need to hunt for food	• ecotourism projects do not always benefit wildlife

Task 4 Doing further research

4.1 **Look at the two websites below for more information on the topic of animal conservation. Find a point that you find useful or interesting, and make notes on it.**

http://www.globalissues.org/article/177/nature-and-animal-conservation
http://www.theguardian.com/environment/endangeredspecies

4.2 Tell your group about it and explain why you find it interesting.

Task 5 Establishing your viewpoint

Once you have thought about the issue and done some background reading, you will be able to establish your own viewpoint (your opinion on the subject). You will have an idea about whether you think endangered species should be protected or not.

5.1 **In three sentences, explain your opinion of animal conservation.**

5.2 **You need to provide evidence to support your opinion(s). What are your arguments for or against animal conservation? Use the information in the articles you have read, as well as ideas and evidence from the poster you made in Unit 2. Draw a table like the one below and make a note of your opinion(s) and the supporting evidence.**

opinion	
supporting evidence	
• explanations	
• arguments relating to your viewpoint	
• examples	
• effects	

5.3 **Work in groups to compare your ideas. Try to come to a consensus (agreement) about your main ideas.**

Reflect

What are the steps needed to prepare successfully for a seminar or a debate? Make a checklist. Which steps do you think would be most difficult for you? Why?

4 Communicating effectively in group discussions

At the end of this unit, you will:

- learn useful language for contributing to academic discussions
- practise using these communication strategies
- evaluate your use of communication strategies

Task 1 Useful language for contributing to group discussions

Your ability to contribute confidently in academic discussions depends on having a wide range of communication strategies. The language you need to use may be more formal, more tentative or more polite than you are accustomed to using in other situations, such as when you are socialising.

1.1 **Look at the categories in the tables. What can you think of to say in these situations?**

stating opinions and summarising
1. giving your opinion about a topic
2. adding something to what has just been said a. (I'd just like to add ...)
3. agreeing with what has been said
4. disagreeing with what has been said
5. summarising what has been said

asking questions in group discussions
1. asking a question
2. asking for repetition, when you haven't heard what has been said
3. asking for clarification, when you haven't completely understood the message

1.2 **Read the expressions and put them in the correct category in the tables in Task 1.1. Compare your answers with a partner's.**

a. ~~I'd just like to add~~ …
b. If I might interrupt for a moment, …
c. X put it very well when he/she said …
d. Could you explain what you meant when you said that …?
e. On balance, …
f. I didn't quite catch that.
g. Excuse me, …
h. I'm afraid I didn't follow your point about … Could you go over that again?
i. You mentioned X, …
j. I see what you mean, but …
k. Could you go over what you said about …?
l. Overall, …
m. I have a question about X.
n. To sum up, …
o. Could you repeat that, please?
p. I would like to ask you something about X.
q. You have a point there, but …
r. I'm afraid I don't agree …
s. X raised some important points.
t. It's true that …, but …
u. I fully agree with X.
v. Can I check that I've understood …?

4

Task 2 Communication strategies in context

2.1 **Read the seven situations (a–g). Write at least two examples of things you could say. Use the expressions from Task 1.2, or any other expressions that you think are appropriate, to help you.**

a. You are distracted because you have just remembered something important you have forgotten to do. You realise that people are looking at you, but you have no idea of what has just been said. What could you say?

b. You are trying hard to follow a complicated argument from a fellow student, but he/she is using technical terminology you have never heard before. What could you say?

c. You completely disagree with the opinions of a speaker. How could you challenge him/her appropriately?

d. You agree with what a speaker has just said, but you have another important point that you wish to add.

e. You feel that you have something really important to add to the discussion. How could you interrupt appropriately in order to make your point?

f. You have been asked to give a summary of what has been discussed. How could you do this?

g. You have forgotten to prepare the text before the discussion, and the text is difficult to understand during the session. What could you say in a group discussion?

Task 3 Practise using communication strategies

You are going to practise using the expressions you have encountered so far, and try out any others that occur to you.

3.1 **Read the statements (a–f) and discuss each one with a partner. Try to use some of the expressions from Task 2. If you can, record your discussion. Otherwise, try to remember which expressions were used.**

a. All education should be free.

b. Making mistakes in English is OK, as long as people understand you.

c. University students should not have part-time jobs.

d. Increasing multiculturalism is a threat to stability.

e. The car is the most dangerous invention ever.

f. Most young people write using computers rather than by hand, so they should be allowed to use computers to write in exams.

3.2 **Think about the language you used in each discussion. Complete the table with the expressions you used. Remember to give reasons for why you agree/disagree.**

agree (reasons)	disagree (reasons)	questions to clarify meaning	follow-up questions for further discussion

4

Task 4 Language activation

4.1 **Check back and review the language from the unit so far. How well can you do the following? Put a tick in the appropriate column.**

communication skills	☺	😐	☹
agree			
disagree			
give reasons and examples			
ask for repetition			
ask a question			
interrupt			
make an excuse			
summarise points			
introduce a topic to a group			
present a basic argument			

4.2 **Work in groups of four. Look at the roles (Person A, B, C and D). Then choose one of the statements from Task 3.1, select roles and discuss the statement for five minutes.**

- Person A will propose a statement and give reasons why they agree with the idea.
- Person B will challenge the statement and give reasons why they disagree with the idea.
- Person C will ask questions to clarify what is being said.
- Person D will ask follow-up questions and take notes.

4.3 **Change roles for your second and third practices. Follow the instructions for your chosen role (Person A, B, C or D) and discuss a different statement for five minutes each.**

Reflect

Which role did you find the easiest? Which was most difficult? Why?
Which communication strategies are you most and least familiar with, and how can you improve in these areas?

5 Encouraging interaction

At the end of this unit, you will be able to:

- identify verbal and non-verbal clues during conversations
- maintain interactive dialogue in discussion
- identify techniques for encouraging or discouraging interaction

Task 1 Using verbal and non-verbal information

When we speak to other people, we give verbal and non-verbal clues to indicate our thoughts and feelings. This can vary from culture to culture, so it is important to identify commonalities and differences.

1.1 **Match the strategies (a–i) with the language clues (1–9).**

Strategies	Language clues
a. Encouraging	1. I think we should develop Yang's idea about …
b. Building on others' ideas	2. I don't believe that's such a good idea.
c. Including all members	3. Why don't we …?
d. Showing agreement	4. Do you think that's possible?
e. Showing disagreement	5. That's a good idea.
f. Asking questions	6. We can conclude that …
g. Making suggestions	7. I agree.
h. Offering information	8. It says here that the most popular form of entertainment is …
i. Summing up	9. Does everyone agree?
• ______	• ______
• ______	• ______
• ______	• ______
• ______	• ______

1.2 **Work in groups to discuss the questions.**

a. Are the strategies used in your culture? If so, how are they signalled?

b. What differences did you discover between the various cultures in your group?

1.3 **In the spaces above, add any more strategies and language clues that you think are important to mention.**

1.4 **Look again at the strategies in Task 1.1 and decide which ones could be communicated in a non-verbal way and how.**

____

____

____

____

____

1.5 **Think of five more strategies that are usually conveyed non-verbally and discuss how that is done.**

a. ______________________________

b. ______________________________

c. ______________________________

d. ______________________________

e. ______________________________

Task 2 Talking at or talking to

2.1 **Work with a partner to discuss the sentences and decide who is talking: a *Type A* or *Type B* person.**

Type A: Talking to you, i.e., prompting a response.
Type B: Talking at you, i.e., not interacting with you.

a. Well, when I was at university, I studied Physics and Maths and now I'm an astrophysicist and I have a successful career ahead of me, which is exciting. ________

b. I'd love to know what you think of your new course. ________

c. You should listen to the new Beyoncé CD. Everyone I know loves it. ________

d. How's your family? ________

e. We've spent enough time on this exercise. Let's do the next one. ________

2.2 **Think about the following questions and how they apply to you. Then discuss your answers with a partner.**

a. Are you more of a Type A or Type B person?

b. Are there any problems with being a Type A person?

c. Might it be useful sometimes to be a Type B person? If so, when?

Task 3 Group behaviour

3.1 Match the strategies (a–g) with the appropriate group behaviour (1–4).

1. Includes shy, quiet people in your group's discussion.
2. Interrupts the conversation.
3. Keeps the floor to himself/herself.
4. Returns the conversation to something you were talking about earlier.

a. Avoids eye contact. 1

b. Says something like 'Can I just come in here?' ___

c. Turns towards another person. ___

d. Says something like 'If I can just finish what I was saying, ...' ___

e. Makes eye contact with the person speaking. ___

f. Says something like 'What do you think about global warming?' ___

g. Says something like 'Back to what I was saying about ...' ___

3.2 Compare your answers in groups. Use the questions to prompt discussion.

- When might it be appropriate to interrupt a conversation?
- Should shy people have to contribute to a team?
- How can you tell whether someone is shy or simply disinterested?
- What's wrong with wanting to talk all the time?

5

Task 4 Listening techniques

4.1 Work in groups. Appoint a note-taker, then discuss which of the following techniques would encourage or discourage someone who was talking. The note-taker will mark the general group consensus in the table.

technique	encourages	discourages	it depends
fidgeting			
maintaining eye contact			
scowling			
smiling			
head nodding			
looking down			
making non-verbal noises, such as *uh-uh* or *mmm*			
using exclamations, such as *Really?!*, *Great!* or *Wow!*			
repeating key speaker words			
asking questions			
keeping silent			
folding your arms across your chest and sitting back in your chair			

4.2 The note-taker will have observed your behaviour during the discussion. Elicit from him/her whether any of these techniques were used during the discussion.

Task 5 Interaction issues

5.1 **Work with a partner to discuss the five situations (a–e).**

What would you do if …

a. … someone you were talking to did not maintain eye contact with you?

b. … someone kept interrupting you?

c. … you felt too shy to join in the conversation?

d. … someone kept using negative body language when talking to you, such as fidgeting, yawning or looking at their watch?

e. … someone asked you a question which you could not answer, in a public place, e.g., in a seminar or a class?

5.2 **Work in groups to discuss one of the aspects of this unit. Try to monitor your own behaviour and that of other students during the discussion.**

Reflect

Reflect on aspects of body language that are used to show interest or disinterest. Which of these techniques do you think you use consciously or subconsciously?

6 Evaluating group performance

At the end of this unit, you will be able to:

- apply communication strategies in a debate
- evaluate your contribution to a discussion
- evaluate your group's performance
- assess development of your teamwork skills

Task 1 Participate in a debate

In Unit 3, you prepared for a debate in your group and in Unit 4 you learned effective communication strategies for academic discussions; now you will put this into practice in the next stage of your group project: participating in a debate.

1.1 **Present your group's views on the project topic:** *Endangered species should be protected*. **Begin by indicating clearly whether your group is for or against the topic. Be prepared to justify your position in a discussion with other students. Each member of the group should contribute.**

Task 2 What kind of contributor am I?

2.1 **Think about your contribution to the debate in Task 1. Evaluate how well you do the activities listed in the table and how you could improve your skills and your performance. Rate yourself, then compare your ratings with a partner's and identify any action you need to take to improve.**

How good am I?	1 = improvement needed, 5 = excellent	action needed
Am I well prepared?		
Do I contribute?		
Am I a good listener?		
Can I argue a point?		
Do I support others?		
Do I ask relevant questions?		
Do I say enough?		
Are my language skills good?		
Do I work well with others?		
Can I do any follow-up tasks?		

You may be formally assessed on your performance, so it is vital that you take the opportunity to participate fully. Tutors may give a mark for both individual and group performance – how much and how well everybody participates in the activity. Group projects help tutors to evaluate students' knowledge as well as their academic skills.

2.2 **Look back at your records of the discussions and meetings you have held as a group for this project. Work through the list below and decide how well you communicate and engage with your group.**

Use a scale of 1 to 5 (1 = I am not confident and the skill needs developing, 5 = I am confident of my ability in this skill).

Student …

a. … arrives on time. ___

b. … has the necessary paperwork with them. ___

c. … has done the required preparation. ___

d. … uses appropriate language strategies, e.g., asks someone to repeat what they have said or to clarify a point. ___

e. … asks relevant questions. ___

f. … agrees and disagrees and can give full reasons. ___

g. … backs up opinions with suitable arguments. ___

h. … listens well. ___

i. … works well with others. ___

j. … takes notes. ___

k. … presents points fluently and uses accurate English. ___

l. … understands the main points of the discussion. ___

m. … does the required homework. ___

n. … is good with technology. ___

2.3 **Which of the points above do you think are most important from the tutor's point of view? Why? List your ideas below.**

- ___
- ___
- ___
- ___
- ___

Task 3 Evaluating group performance

You will have discovered that working collaboratively in a group presents challenges, but it also provides opportunities for deeper learning. The group project skills that you develop at university will be greatly valued in your future career. It is worthwhile, therefore, to self-assess the effectiveness of your group performance regularly and note how you are developing these lifelong skills.

Evaluate your own input to each group project you undertake and evaluate the work of the group as a whole.

3.1 **How did your group perform as a whole? Complete the table. In the 'comments' column, give examples to illustrate your response.**

	evaluation	comments
How effectively did you collaborate together?		
How much support did you provide for each other?		
What went well?		
What went badly?		
What have you learned from this experience?		

3.2 **Compare your answers with a partner's. In what ways were they the same or different?**

3.3 Evaluate your own input to the group project.

a. Name three things you did well.

1. ____________________
2. ____________________
3. ____________________

b. Name three things you didn't do so well.

1. ____________________
2. ____________________
3. ____________________

3.4 How could you improve the contribution you made to your group?

- ____________________
- ____________________
- ____________________
- ____________________
- ____________________

3.5 How do you feel about the group activities you have completed?
Use a scale of 1 to 5 (1 = negative, 5 = positive). Then explain why you chose this number.

negative 1 — 2 — 3 — 4 — 5 positive

____

Task 4 Developing your teamwork stills

4.1 **Consider the skills you are developing by participating in collaborative projects.**

Use a scale of 1 to 5 (1 = I am not confident and the skill needs developing, 5 = I am confident of my ability in this skill).

a. I understand my role and responsibilities within the team and fulfil these to the best of my ability. ___

b. I can retain a clear vision of the group's goals and objectives as the project develops. ___

c. I understand that planning is an essential part of group work and I participate actively in planning meetings. ___

d. I can prioritise my tasks and complete these on time. ___

e. I respect others in the group and support them. ___

f. I deliver what I have agreed to do, on time. ___

g. I can communicate honestly and sensitively to my fellow team members. ___

h. I see mistakes as an opportunity to learn and can accept constructive criticism. ___

i. I work towards the goals agreed by the group. ___

j. I understand and keep to the ground rules set by the group. ___

Reflect

Now you have had the opportunity to engage in a group project, consider the statements about teamwork. Do you agree with them? Why/Why not?

a. Two heads are better than one.

b. TEAM = Together Everyone Achieves More.

c. There is no 'I' in teamwork.

d. A successful team beats with one heart.

e. Real teams don't emerge unless individuals in them take risks involving conflict, trust, interdependence and hard work.

Web work

Website 1

Learn Higher

http://archive.learnhigher.ac.uk/groupwork/

Review

'Learn Higher' is a site designed by three Learn Higher partners, the Universities of Brunel, Bradford and Leeds, to help students understand and overcome the challenges of group work.
It includes a series of ten video episodes, taking five students through the journey of a group work project.

Task

Click on 'The episodes' tab and watch 'Episode 1 – The first meeting'. Then go to the 'Episode analysis' page and watch this version, where the students conduct the initial meeting in a more positive and productive way. Discuss the differences in behaviour you note.

Website 2

Prepare for Success

http://www.prepareforsuccess.org.uk/

Review

'Prepare for Success' is an interactive web learning tool for international students developed by the University of Southampton and the UK Council for International Student Affairs (UKCISA). There are 23 units, each covering a different topic, to help students find out about different aspects of academic life in the UK and the skills needed for effective study.

Task

Click on Unit 20 'Working with others'. Read through the instructions and find out the kind of skills that students need to work together effectively.

Complete the 'Skills for collaborating' activity and check your answers by clicking the 'Show feedback' icon.

Extension activities

Activity 1

Reflect on the various tasks that you have completed in this module.

a. List three skills that contribute to effective group work.

1. ______________________________
2. ______________________________
3. ______________________________

b. List three things that contribute to poor group work.

1. ______________________________
2. ______________________________
3. ______________________________

Activity 2

a. **Reflect on the various group activities you have participated in.**
   - What did you find most difficult or challenging?
   - What did you find came naturally?

b. **Make a quick note of the skills that other members of your team noticed in you.**
   - Which skills do you need to improve on?

Activity 3

Write a report of up to 500 words reflecting on the processes and outcomes of the project. Your report should address the following question: *To what extent was your experience of working in a group successful?*

Glossary

active listening (n) Listening in a way that shows you are giving your full attention to the speaker. The listener is able to demonstrate comprehension and give the speaker the impression that he/she is being understood.

analyse (v) To break an issue down into parts in order to study, identify and discuss their meaning and/or relevance.

assess (v) To make a judgement about somebody or something. For example, you will have to assess the contributions made by yourself and other members of a group after completing a group project.

assessment (n) A judgement or opinion about somebody or something.

body language (n) A form of non-verbal communication of feelings and ideas through movements of the body. For example, certain body movements such as fidgeting and yawning may indicate boredom.

brainstorm (v) The act of writing down all the thoughts and ideas you have about a topic without stopping to monitor, edit or organise them. Brainstorming is a creative process that can be done alone or in a group.

characteristic (n) Unique feature or trait that characterises a person, thing, place or group and identifies it.

collaborate (v) To work together with another person (or other people) on a project or assignment.

communication skills/strategies (n) Skills and techniques that enable you to listen, talk and write to other people effectively. Good communication skills allow you to make a positive impression, participate well in discussions and convey ideas clearly.

conflict (n) (v) 1 (n) Strong opposition or disagreement within a group or between two or more groups. 2 (v) To clash or have opposing ideas or points of view.

consensus (n) An agreement or majority decision reached by a group.

contribute (v) To actively take part in something or give something to a situation, such as time, energy, thought or money. For example, it is important to contribute ideas when working in a team.

culture (n) The beliefs, institutions, traditions, arts and patterns of behaviour of a particular group of people that help them structure their lives.

debate (n) (v) 1 (n) A formal discussion, often about serious issues or problems. A debate is structured so that speakers with opposing viewpoints take turns to state their opinions and answer questions in front of an audience. 2 (v) To participate in a discussion with someone who has an opposing viewpoint.

discourage (v) To try to prevent someone from doing something through words or actions such as gesture and facial expression.

dominate (v) To have a controlling position in a group or strong influence on a situation.

encourage (v) To support someone and give him/her confidence to do something through words or actions such as gestures and facial expression.

evaluate (v) To assess information in terms of quality, relevance, objectivity and accuracy.

eye contact (n) A form of non-verbal communication in which people look into, or avoid looking into, each other's eyes when they communicate.

goal (n) An aim or end purpose that someone tries to achieve or reach.

higher education (n) Tertiary education that is beyond the level of secondary education and usually offers first and higher degrees. A university is an institution of higher education.

interaction (n) How people or things act together with each other, respond to and affect each other.

interrupt (v) To enter a conversation or situation without waiting for someone to finish speaking or doing something.

lecture (n) A formal talk or presentation given to inform or instruct people. In tertiary education, lectures are usually delivered by academic staff to large groups of students.

multicultural (adj) Describes a community or group that is made up of individuals of different national, racial or religious backgrounds.

non-verbal communication (n) The communication of ideas (intentionally or unintentionally) through behaviour, body movement, gestures and facial expression, but not through words.

objective (adj) (n) 1 (adj) Not influenced by personal feelings or emotions. 2 (n) The aim, or what you want to achieve from an activity.

opinion (n) A personal belief that may be subjective and is not based on certainty or fact.

outcome (n) A final decision and result.

participate (v) To get involved or take part in something. For example, it is important to participate actively in debates and seminars.

peer (n) A person who is the same age or who has the same social status as you.

peer assessment (n) To assess the contributions made by other members of the group.

presentation (n) A short lecture, talk or demonstration given in front of an audience. The speaker prepares his or her presentation in advance and will often use visual aids or realia to illustrate it.

prioritise (v) To put tasks in order of importance to ensure that you complete everything on time.

research (n) (v) 1 (n) Information collected from a variety of sources about a specific topic. 2 (v) To gather information from a variety of sources and analyse and compare it.

role (n) The part someone plays in a group (or any situation that involves interacting with other people). In some situations, these roles may be flexible or unspoken, in others, they are well-defined, such as the leader of a team.

self-evaluation (n) The process of testing and assessing your own performance or progress in order to decide which areas you need to work on and/or select for future study or employment.

seminar (n) A small group discussion led by a tutor, lecturer or guest speaker. Students are expected to take an active part in the seminar and may be asked to lead the seminar.

strategy (n) A plan of action that you follow when you want to achieve a particular goal. For example, it is possible to have a clear strategy for passing an exam.

teamworking skills (n) The skills needed to participate effectively as a member of a group, a team or a network. They include the following abilities: to work constructively with others, to be assertive without dominating too much, to be flexible and to contribute ideas.

technique (n) A method or way of doing something that involves skill and/or efficiency. For example, it is possible to learn useful techniques for answering exam questions.

time management (n) The ability to organise your time so that you use it more effectively and efficiently.

Notes

Published by
Garnet Publishing Ltd.
8 Southern Court
South Street
Reading RG1 4QS, UK

This book is based on an original concept devised by Dr Anthony Manning and Mrs Frances Russell.

ISBN 978 1 78260 177 7

British Library Cataloguing-in-Publication Data
A catalogue record for this book is available from the British Library.

Production

Project manager: Clare Chandler
Editorial team: Clare Chandler, Kate Kemp
Design & Layout: Simon Ellway, Madeleine Maddock
Photography: iStockphoto

Garnet Publishing and the authors of TASK would like to thank the staff and students of the International Foundation Programme at the University of Reading for their respective roles in the development of these teaching materials.

Garnet Publishing would like to thank Jennifer Book and Paul Harvey for their contribution to the First edition of the TASK series.

All website URLs provided in this publication were correct at the time of printing. If any URL does not work, please contact your tutor, who will help you find similar resources.

Printed and bound in Lebanon by International Press: interpress@int-press.com

Acknowledgements

Page 7: Task 4, *Project Brief: Endangered Species*, adapted from a project task and reproduced with kind permission of Jonathan Smith.

Page 16: Task 2.3, *Wildlife conservation projects do more harm than good, says expert*, reproduced with kind permission of The Guardian.

Transferable Academic Skills Kit **TASK**

Group Work & Projects

University Foundation Study

The **Transferable Academic Skills Kit (TASK)** is a flexible learning resource that has been carefully designed to develop the key transferable skills that promote students' success in university and college study. Whether you are a student or a teacher, the TASK series provides a tried and tested teaching and learning tool suitable for a broad range of academic disciplines.

A series of supported exercises relates theory to practice and provides students with the tools to develop a framework of skills that can then be used in a wide range of contexts, both inside and outside the academic world. Each module also has web work and extension activities that offer additional information and practice relating to the skills covered in that module.

TASK can be followed as a complete course or individual modules can be selected to address specific needs, building the skills required by home and international students at all levels.

The series has been created by members of the International Foundation Programme, provided by the International Study and Language Institute (ISLI) at the University of Reading.

The complete TASK series comprises:

1. Academic Culture
2. Group Work & Projects
3. Critical Thinking
4. Essay Writing
5. Scientific Writing
6. Research & Online Sources
7. Referencing & Avoiding Plagiarism
8. Presentations
9. Assessments, Exams & Revision
10. Numeracy

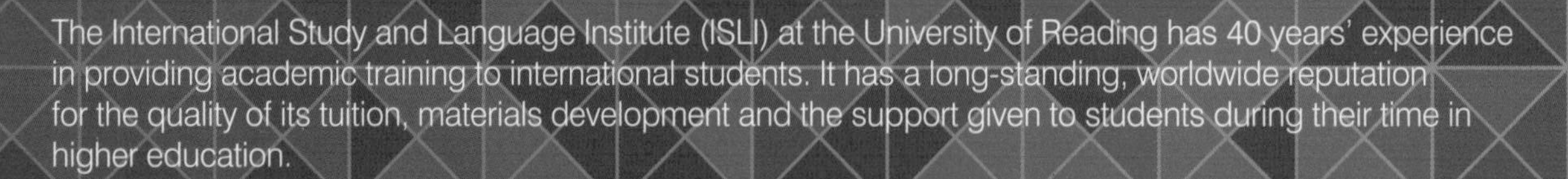

The International Study and Language Institute (ISLI) at the University of Reading has 40 years' experience in providing academic training to international students. It has a long-standing, worldwide reputation for the quality of its tuition, materials development and the support given to students during their time in higher education.

ISBN 978-1-78260-177-7
9 781782 601777 >

www.garneteducation.com

5

Transferable Academic Skills Kit **TASK**

University Foundation Study

Scientific Writing

Student's Book